I0139779

USE YOUR MANNERS

Based on the "Manners" song written
and performed by Bridgette Johnson (DJ B.J.)

Illustrated by Derrick Thomas
& Israel Arellano

Contact Information
bblessedjohnson@gmail.com
+502-776-2126

For Orders
Bridgette Johnson
+502-502-776-2126

ISBN:978-0-692-93406-7
LCCN: 2017913366
Book Layout Design: Glory ePublishing Services
Illustrations: Israel Arellano and Derrick Thomas

"All Rights Reserved. No part of this book may be reproduced or utilized in any form or by any means, electronic or mechanical, including photocopying, recording, or by any information storage and retrieval system, without permission in writing from the Author."
© Copyright 2017, Bridgette Johnson

Hello boys and girls,

I am **DJ B.J.**, and I want to speak with you about **Good Manners!**

What are Manners you may ask?

Simply put Manners are ways of behaving around and acting toward others.

There are both Good manners and Bad manners.

Learning Good manners will give you confidence and make you more pleasant to be around.

If you are being respectful and considerate of others, you will often get the same treatment in return.

Manners are an important social skill that is necessary for people to live together.

People and Children with BAD MANNERS not only offend others, but BAD MANNERS can reflect badly on their parents.

Showing consideration for other people's feelings is an important part of developing GOOD MANNERS.

Learning to apologize when you have hurt or offended someone helps you to remember to think about other people's feelings. Apologizing is also a way of smoothing over an argument without an adult's intervention.

Above all be Considerate!

It's important to remember not to do things to other people that you don't like having done to yourself. If you do something rude or mean to anyone, think about how it would feel to have the same thing the done to you.

Always try to be considerate, such as holding doors for people, being polite at the table and showing good sportsmanship whether you win or lose.

MARTIN, WE LOVE YOU. HAVE A GREAT FIRST DAY.

MAKE LOTS OF NEW FRIENDS AT COURTESY ELEMENTARY.

ALWAYS STOP, LOOK, AND LISTEN! SO YOU CAN BE AWARE OF YOUR

SURROUNDINGS.

MOST OF ALL REMEMBER TO USE YOUR MANNERS TO SHOW RESPECT.

HAVING RESPECT WILL LEAVE A GOOD IMPRESSION WITH THE TEACHERS,

AND YOUR FRIENDS. "YES MAM", SAID MARTIN MANNERS.

WITH GREAT ANTICIPATION, MARTIN COULDN'T WAIT TO MEET SOME OF HIS NEW CLASSMATES.

BEFORE HE COULD REACH THE BUS STOP,

THERE WAS A FLASHING BRIGHT RED ELECTRO-MAGNETIC SIGNAL THAT APPEARED ON HIS SHIRT. OH NO! SOMETHING DISRESPECTFUL MUST BE TAKING PLACE.

MY PARENTS HAVE TAUGHT ME STRONG VALUES OF RESPECTFULNESS, TO THE DEGREE THAT I TRANSFORM INTO

Mighty Manners, the Super Hero of all good deeds.

URRR! URRR! URRR!

MY ELECTRO-MAGNETIC SUPER POWERS ARE COMING ALIVE.

LOOK! MY M&M IS GETTING A RED SIGNAL.

IMMEDIATELY, I MUST STOP, LOOK, AND LISTEN! .

SHHHHH!

I CAN HEAR THE SOUND OF SOMEONE SAYING, "HELP!!! I AM BEING BULLIED!"

I AM MIGHTY MANNERS AND I AM HERE TO SAY I DON'T LIKE BAD MANNERS AND I AM ON MY WAY..

MEANWHILE........AT THE BUS STOP.

"MOVE OUT OF THE WAY, YOU SLIMY FACE MORON!

I AM ALWAYS THE FIRST ONE TO GET ON THE BUS."

"NO WAY, HOSEA," SAID JASON. "I AM NOT BUDGING."

"MOVE OUT OF THE WAY!

YOU KNOW I AM THE BOSS, APPLESAUCE," SAID BUSTER.

"WELL, THREATEN ME IF YOU WANT TO.

I'M NOT MOVING, YOU GOODY HUNK OF NOTHING," SAID JASON.

"JASON, WE ARE SO PROUD OF YOU.

YOU STOOD UP TO BUSTER THE BULLY," SAID MARIA.

YOU ARE A HERO!

"THE STUDENT HANDBOOK SAID WE LINE UP AND WE KEEP OUR HANDS TO

OURSELVES.

WE STAND WITH YOU JASON. WE ARE NOT MOVING!

WE WERE HERE FIRST.

BESIDES THAT, AT *COURTESY* ELEMENTARY,

THERE IS *ZERO TOLERANCE* FOR BULLYING.

NOW GET IN THE BACK OF THE LINE, BUSTER!"

"OKAY, MR. PIE FACE! SAID BUSTER

I TOLD YOU WHEN I SPEAK, EVERYBODY LISTENS.

SINCE YOU WON'T MOVE OUT OF THE WAY,

TAKE THIS FIST TO YOUR BIG NOSE, IS WHAT I SAY."

BAM! BAM! UMF!

"AWWWWH, MAN!

HE HIT ME IN THE NOSE.

SOMEBODY HELPPPP!!

HELPPPP!!

I AM BEING BULLIED!"

BAM! BAM! BOOM!

CRASH!

"HELPPPP!

I BELIEVE MY NOSE IS BROKEN.

MAYBE I SHOULDN'T HAVE SPOKEN

UP.

THIS IS A JOB FOR *MIGHTY MANNERS*," SAID JASON.

"HAH! HAH! HAH! WHAT CAN MIGHTY MANNERS DO?

I CAN ROLL HIM OVER WITH BOTH OF MY SHOES.

I *RULE* THIS BUS STOP!"

CHHHHHHHH!

CHHHHHHHH!

MY ELECTRO-MAGNETIC RAYS ENABLE ME TO SOAR AS FAST AS
LIGHTNING BOLTS.

ZOOM, ZAP, KAZOON!!!

I MUST GO TO THE SCENE REAL SOON,

BEFORE SOMEONE GETS HURT.

HELP ME COUNT DOWN, 5,4,3,2,1!

BLAST OFF!

CHHHHHHHH!

"**ALRIGHT**, BUSTER!

ENOUGH IS ENOUGH!

MOVE OUT OF THE WAY, BULLY! YOU'RE NOT SO TOUGH!

ALL YOU DO IS MAKE A BIG BLUFF," SAID MIGHTY MANNERS.

"OKAY! OKAY! I WILL STOP."

IT'S TIME SOMEONE TAUGHT YOU ABOUT **MANNERS**.

I AM **MIGHTY MANNERS**, AND I AM HERE TO SAY

YOU DON'T EVER TREAT YOUR FRIENDS THIS WAY.

"WHEN YOU SHOUT AND BOSS EVERYBODY AROUND,

THAT MAKES YOU LOOK LIKE A CLOWN.

WHEN YOU ARE RUDE,

NO ONE WILL LIKE YOU, DUDE."

"I AM REALLY ASHAMED OF MY ACTIONS," SAID BUSTER.

"I DON'T WANT TO BE A BULLY.

I JUST WANT TO BE POPULAR."

"JUST USE YOUR **MANNERS TO SHOW RESPECT**, AND YOU WILL BE

POPULAR."

"IT'S WRONG TO BULLY

ANYBODY," SAID BUSTER.

I AM GOING TO MAKE AN APOLOGY TO ALL MY FRIENDS.

I LEARNED SOMETHING NEW TODAY FROM *MIGHTY MANNERS...*

TO SHOW RESPECT.

NEXT TIME I WILL GET IN LINE QUIETLY AND KEEP MY HANDS TO

MYSELF."

"BUSTER, LISTEN CAREFULLY.

A GOOD APOLOGY ACCEPTS RESPONSIBILITY. IT PROVIDES REAL DETAILS

ABOUT WHAT HAPPENED

AND WHAT YOU'RE DOING TO PREVENT IT FROM HAPPENING AGAIN," SAID

MIGHTY MANNERS.

"I AM **MIGHTY MANNERS**, AND I AM HERE TO SAY,

FRIENDS ARE SUPPOSED TO GET ALONG LIKE THIS EVERY DAY.

I HELP CHILDREN LEARN FROM THEIR MISTAKES.

I USE SITUATIONS LIKE BULLYING AS 'TEACHABLE MOMENTS' TO

REINFORCE GOOD DEEDS.

HAVE A GREAT DAY AT SCHOOL TODAY,

BOYS AND GIRLS.

ALWAYS REMEMBER TO USE YOUR **MANNERS** TO SHOW **RESPECT**."

URRR!   *URRR!*   *URRR!*

MY ELECTRO-MAGNETIC SUPER POWERS ARE COMING ALIVE!

LOOK, MY M&M IS GETTING A SIGNAL.

IMMEDIATELY, I MUST *STOP,* *LOOK,* AND LISTEN! .

SHHHHHH!

I CAN HEAR THE SOUND OF SOMEONE DISRESPECTING AN ADULT.

I AM *MIGHTY MANNERS*, AND I AM HERE TO SAY,

I DON'T LIKE *BAD MANNERS*

I AM ON MY WAY!

MR. RODRIGUEZ REVIEWED THE EXPECTATIONS FOR THE

LUNCHROOM

WITH TWO STUDENTS.

HE REMINDED THEM TO USE THEIR INDOOR VOICES AND WALKING FEET

BEFORE ENTERING THE LUNCHROOM.

AS HE WAS TALKING, HE TURNED AROUND AND NOTICED RYAN WITH FOOD

SPLATTERED ALL OVER HIS FACE.

" EXCUSE ME, BOYS, WHILE I GET A NAPKIN FOR YOUR FRIEND RYAN,"

"MR. RODRIGUEZ, YOU ARE ALWAYS SO HELPFUL.

WE WANT TO BE JUST LIKE YOU WHEN WE GROW UP."

"HERE YOU GO, RYAN."

"GIVE ME THAT NAPKIN! OLD MAN RODRIGUEZ. I NEED IT TO WIPE MY FACE."

"RYAN, HAS ANYONE EVER TAUGHT YOU THAT SNATCHING IS NOT NICE?"

"I CAN SNATCH WHATEVER I WANT, AND THERE ISN'T ANYTHING YOU CAN DO ABOUT IT!"

"YOU NEED TO LEARN THE CORRECT WAY TO TALK TO ADULTS WHEN THEY ARE TRYING TO HELP YOU."

"WHATEVER!" SAID RYAN.

MR. RODRIGUEZ BOWED HIS HEAD

AND SAID,

"THIS IS A JOB FOR *MIGHTY MANNERS!*"

CHHHHHHHH!

MY ELECTRO-MAGNETIC RAYS EMPOWER ME TO SOAR AS FAST AS

LIGHTNING BOLTS.

ZOOM, ZAP, KAZOON,!!!

I MUST GO TO THE SCENE REAL SOON,

BEFORE SOMEONE GETS UPSET.

HELP ME COUNTDOWN, 5,4,3,2,1.

BLAST OFF!

CHHHHHHHH!

"RYAN, I JUST GOT A **RED** FLASH ALERT ON MY **M&M** BADGE.

YOU SNATCHED A NAPKIN FROM AN ADULT'S HAND WITHOUT SAYING,

"THANK YOU".

MR. RODRIGUEZ DIDN'T HAVE TO BE NICE TO YOU.

HE SAW THE FOOD ALL OVER YOUR FACE.

HE WENT TO GET A NAPKIN FOR YOU.

WHEN ANYONE GIVES YOU SOMETHING, ALWAYS SAY, *"THANK YOU"*.

THAT'S CALLED *"GOOD MANNERS"*.

"MR. RODRIGUEZ, I AM VERY SORRY FOR SNATCHING THAT NAPKIN.

THANK YOU".

"YOU'RE WELCOME."

URRRR!   *URRRR!*   *URRRR!*

"MY ELECTRO-MAGNETIC SUPER POWERS ARE COMING ALIVE.

IMMEDIATELY I MUST *STOP,* *LOOK,* AND *LISTEN!* .

SHHHHH!

I CAN HEAR A YOUNG BOY GETTING ANGRY AND SPITTING ON HIS

CLASSMATE ON THE PLAYGROUND.

I AM **MIGHTY MANNERS**, AND I AM HERE TO SAY

I DON'T LIKE **bad manners.**

I AM ON MY WAY!"

AFTER LUNCH............

OKAY!

"ARE YOU READY KIDS"?

"YES, TEACHER".

"IT'S TIME FOR RECESS, LET'S GO OVER THE EXPECTATIONS BEFORE WE GO:

USE YOUR MANNERS.

SHARE WITH ONE ANOTHER.

TAKE TURNS.

CLEAN UP YOUR AREA.

CLASS LET'S HAVE FUN OUTSIDE AND PLAY TOGETHER AS A TEAM."

"YEEA! YEEA! WE LOVE PLAYING WITH OUR FRIENDS, MRS. JAMIESON."

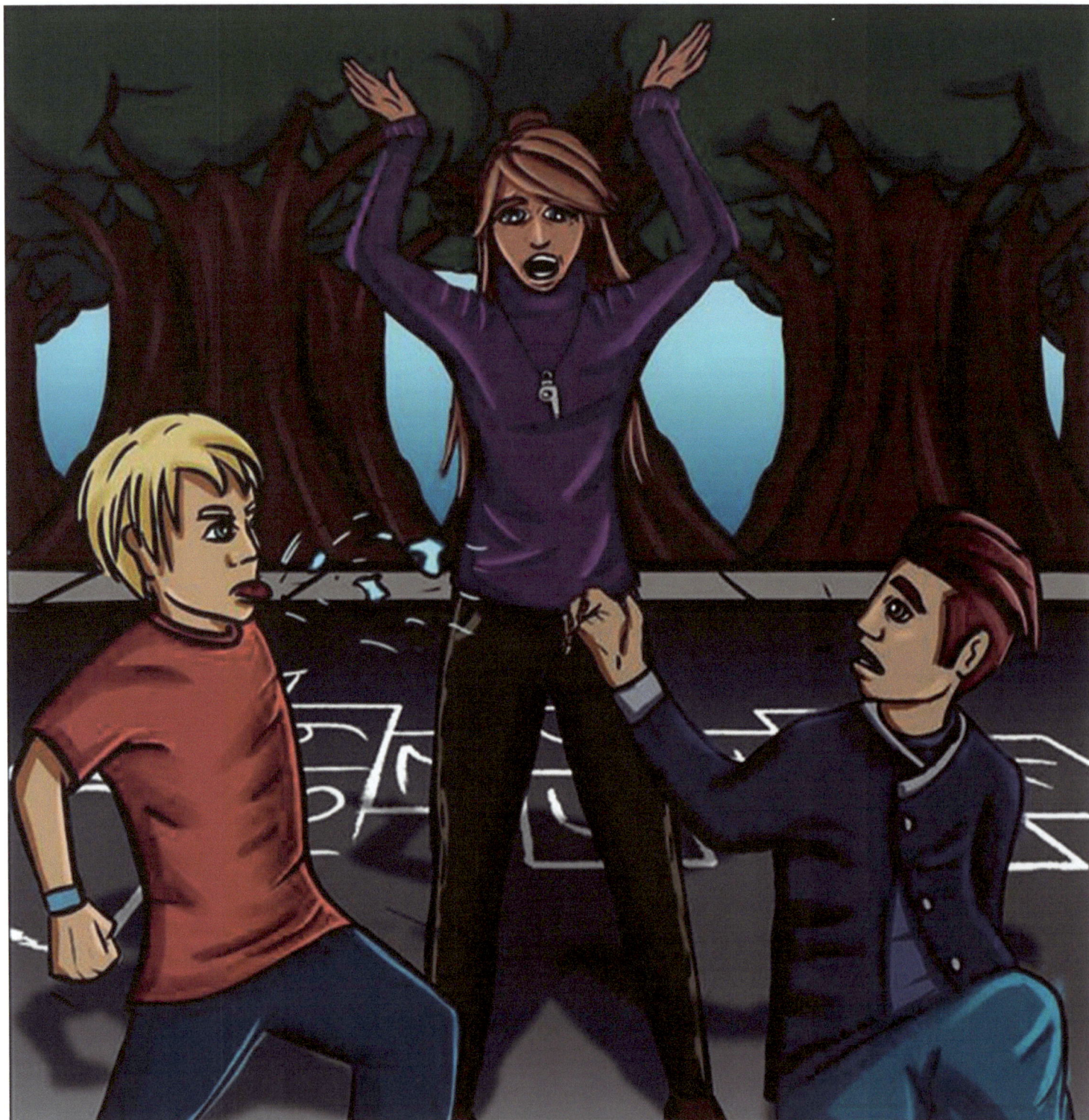

ON THE PLAYGROUND..........

"HEYYY! BOYS.

WHAT HAPPENED? WE JUST READ THE RULES.

REMEMBER?

SHARE OUR CHALK.

TAKE TURNS."

"HE WON'T SHARE! I HAVE ASKED HIM THREE TIMES....

NOW WATCH THIS. HERE IT GOES. PUH! PUH! PHEWW!"

"OH! OH! NO! CHICO, DON'T SPIT ON GREGORY," SAID MRS. JAMIESON.

"AWHHHH! THESE KIDS

ARE NOT LISTENING!

I SURRENDER.

THIS IS A JOB FOR *MIGHTY MANNERS."*

CHHHHHHHH!

CHHHHHHHH!

MY ELECTRO-MAGNETIC RAYS EMPOWER ME TO SOAR AS FAST AS

LIGHTNING BOLTS.

ZOOM, ZAP, KAZOON,!!!

I MUST GO TO THE SCENE REAL SOON,

BEFORE SOMEONE GETS HURT.

HELP ME COUNTDOWN, 5,4,3,2,1.

BLAST OFF!

CHHHHHHHH!

"CHICO CAN YOU EXPLAIN WHY SPIT IS ON GREGORY'S CLOTHES?"

"I TOLD HIM TO GIVE ME THE CHALK, AND

HE WOULDN'T.

SO, I SPIT ON HIM TO MAKE HIM DO IT."

"SPITTING IS UNACCEPTABLE," SAID MIGHTY MANNERS.

"THERE ARE OTHER WAYS TO RELEASE YOUR FRUSTRATION.

LOOK AT HIS NEW JACKET. IT'S RUINED."

"UH! UH! I AM STARTING TO FEEL TERRIBLY BAD," SAID CHICO.

"SPITTING IS VERY NASTY.

I WILL HELP CLEAN IT OFF HIS JACKET."

MIGHTY MANNERS SAID, "SHARING AND TAKING TURNS WILL HELP TO

PREVENT THIS PROBLEM FROM HAPPENING AGAIN".

Mighty Manners
AKA
"Martin Manners"

"FAREWELL MY FRIENDS!

IT HAS BEEN A LONG DAY OF *TEACHING GOOD DEEDS*.

IT'S GETTING LATE.

MY PARENTS ARE PROBABLY WORRIED ABOUT ME.

I WILL GO HOME AS MARTIN MANNERS, REST A LITTLE BIT,

AND WAKE UP TO ANOTHER DAY OF HEROIC ADVENTURES.

BEFORE I GO, HELP ME TO SING, "*USE YOUR MANNERS*".

REMEMBER TO KEEP THIS SONG IN YOUR HEART, WHEREVER YOU GO".

"Use My Manners"

I use my manners to show respect.

I use my manners to show respect.

I use my manners to show respect,

when I use my manners.

Children saying thank you, thank you, thank you,

Children saying thank you, thank you, thank you,

Children saying thank you, thank you, thank you,

When they use their manners.

When anyone gives me something, I say "thank you".

When I say it so politely, they will really, really like me.

Children saying yes ma'am, yes ma'am, yes ma'am,

Children saying, yes ma'am, yes ma'am, yes ma'am,

Children saying yes ma'am, yes ma'am, yes ma'am,

When they use their manners.

When my mother talks to me, I say," Yes ma'am".

When I say it so politely, they will really, really like me.

Children saying yes sir, yes sir, yes sir,

Children saying yes sir, yes sir, yes sir,

Children saying yes sir, yes sir, yes sir,

When they use their manners.

When my father calls my name, I say, "Yes sir".

When I say it so politely, they will really really like me.

Children saying excuse me, excuse me, excuse me,

Children saying excuse me, excuse me, excuse me,

Children saying excuse me, excuse me, excuse me,

When they use their manners.

When I bump into someone, I always say, "Excuse me".

When I say it so politely, they will really, really like me.

Children saying, I'm sorry, I'm sorry, I'm sorry,

Children saying I'm sorry, I'm sorry, I'm sorry,

Children saying I'm sorry, I'm sorry, I'm sorry,

When they use their manners.

When I accidentally bump into someone, I always say, "I'm sorry".

When I say it so politely, they will really, really like me.

Children saying please, please, please,

Children saying please, please, please,

Children saying please, please, please,

When they use their manners.

When I want something, I always say, "Please".

When I say it so politely, they will really, really like me.

I use my manners to show respect.

I use my manners to show respect.

I use my manners to show respect,

When I use my manners.

I use my manners to show respect.

I use my manners to show respect.

I use my manners to show respect,

When I use my manners.

M₃ A₁ N₁ N₁ E₁ R₁ S₁

SPELLS MANNERS.

M₃ A₁ N₁ N₁ E₁ R₁ S₁

SPELLS MANNERS.

Until the next adventure be on the 👀 lookout for anti-manners!

ETTA-KITT

"AKA Angel Vasquez"

"HELLO, MY NAME IS ANGEL VASQUEZ AKA 'ETTA-KITT'.

I AM GOING TO SHOW YOU

HOW YOU CAN USE PROPER ETIQUETTE

EVERYWHERE YOU GO.

WHAT IS ETIQUETTE, YOU MIGHT ASK?

IT IS THE RULES THAT TELL YOU THE PROPER AND POLITE WAY TO

BEHAVE."

FOR AN EXAMPLE:

NEVER TALK WITH YOUR MOUTH FULL.

CHEW WITH YOUR MOUTH CLOSED.

WIPE YOUR FACE WITH A NAPKIN.

SAY "PLEASE" AND "THANK YOU".

ASK FOR WHAT YOU NEED IN A NICE VOICE TONE.

About The Author

Bridgette Johnson Owner of CreativelyIn-vented LLC. Bachelor's Degree in Early Childhood Education. Teacher in Jefferson County School System for over 17 years. Very passionate about working with children and seeing them learn in creative new ways. "Use Your Manners" is her second to market book with CD. Recently appeared on a local T.V. show Dream Funders. Known as DJ B.J. the rapping school teacher in her first book, Hey! Hey! I Know My Five Senses. She does live musical stage performances for children around the city of Louisville Kentucky.

Dedication

I dedicate this book to my precious grandchildren Dior, Kamani, Brandon.

Acknowledgements

I want to acknowledge God for the many gifts and talents he has bestowed on me. My husband Kevin Johnson and my children Kaila, Jeremy, Kevin Jr. Dominque and Ramon who help support my project.

www.ingramcontent.com/pod-product-compliance
Lightning Source LLC
Chambersburg PA
CBHW041426090426
42741CB00002B/50